(The 7 Virtuous Business Woman Slayers)

Slayers)

(7 Deadly Copouts)

_____

(Tammie T. Polk)

(The 7 Virtuous Business Woman Slayers)
Copyright © 2016 by (Tammie T. Polk)

ISBN-13:
978-1535126816

ISBN-10:
1535126817

Cover Design by AngelArts
www.angelarts.biz

Dedication

This book is dedicated to any woman who has ever been at a standstill...for the ones who want to do, have, and be more yet feel like life is literally standing in their way...for the ones who just can't seem to wrap their heads around what is going on in their world and just want I to end...for those who have a heap of ashes piled on top of a treasure that's dying to get out...this one is for you!

I want to thank my cover designer and dear friend, Dana, for believing in and helping me with yet another project; my mentor and heart sister, Tameka, for being there and listening; my dear friend Suzanne, for giving me a chance; my family, for putting up with me writing another one; and to all who support me, I love you more than words can say!

Table of Contents

Foreword by
Suzanne Taylor-King

I remember the day like it was yesterday, the day that I realized every excuse had been used up and I was just plain out of them. It was a day that seemed pretty normal to me, my son was at school, the cleaning and laundry were done, so I sat down to work and record a podcast episode, and I interviewed a woman that changed the trajectory of my life. Through all my excuses for why my business was not accomplishing my mission, not making me a decent income, might even be costing me money some months just to hold up the appearance of having a business ……. what did I really have back then? I had a fancy hobby that I called my business, that was actually costing me money every month! Imagine being in "business" for years, being "known" as the expert in your town, having a great website, social media following but not generating any sales! That is exactly the spot I was stuck in…. I was being slain by every excuse in this book! I was afraid to ask for money or payment, this coming from a childhood "creediness" comment of my mother's. What comments are you holding onto from childhood, a past relationship? It was not until I realized the power of positive psychology, affirmations, confidence and told myself to stop the bull#!%! and get moving that things started to happen. Instead of just saying I am a Holistic Life Coach I was able to step into my gifts and say that I empower women's inner healing abilities through essential oils, nutrition and energy work. To truly share my story with my friends, family and followers, to not be afraid of sharing my gifts, talents and energy with others. To know that my great work needs to be supported and so does yours! Be confidant, be strong, be open, be virtuous and most of all have no excuses……nothing can hold you back except that person inside your head that says you can't. Step out of your head and into your heart, and say "In deep gratitude and for the benefit of all beings, infinite riches, perfect health and harmony flow freely into my life now." every morning and every evening and it just might change your excuses into affirmations.

Thank you Tammie helping me navigate a "fork" in my road to success and happiness.

Suzanne Taylor-King RDH, HLC, CWC, CPC
Founder & CEO Taylor'd Wellness Associates
Healthy Living Designer
Aromatherapy/Reiki/Reflexology Positive
Psychology Practitioner

Foreword by
Tameka Anderson

This book, "The 7 Virtuous Business Woman Slayers" written by Tammie Polk describes a lot of the places I found myself in as a woman. It made me chuckle to myself because just reading the first slayer and hearing Tammie's story about starting her business with $700 and a stack of business cards leads me to let you know why this book is necessary.

I chuckled when I heard Tammie's story about starting her business with only $700 because I had less than that when I started my business. I was a single mother and don't even think that I was earning $700 per two-week pay period when I started my business. I was a cashier at Sam's Club (before you start to laugh let me explain why I chose that occupation) and I knew I wanted out. I wanted to work for myself and didn't know how to make it happen with zero dollars and zero cents.

I was broke.

All I had was a creative brain, some awesome ideas, and children—a lot of them. Good thing for me the business I wanted to start involved children so this worked out in my favor. Back to why I chose to be a cashier at Sam's Club. I chose that job specifically for the purpose of speaking with business owners. I knew when they shopped there they had to see me before leaving the store so my mission was simple, speak with EVERY business owner who checked out in my lane. Yes, every, single one of them. I knew that I didn't have time or money to pay for business advice so I used my creative brain to pick the brains of the business owners daily while I earned my paycheck.

Working as that cashier to business owners was the best thing I could have done for myself because as I was working I was learning that it didn't take money to make money, it took creativity and ingenuity and boy did I have a LOT of both. After listening to the business owners I was told there were two things I needed in order to start my business; I needed customers and I needed a location. So putting my creative brain to work, I knew I didn't have money to advertise so I had to find someone who would advertise for me.

I approached my local community center about partnering with them to offer a program to teach youth how to boost confidence through performing arts. They had both the location and customers and needed more programming so it was a win-win for everyone. I got my first contract before I even had a business license. I had a class full of paying students and I incurred no upfront costs. Can you say creativity and ingenuity?

Now fast forward 7 years and I am a pillar in my community for children and parents. I host much anticipated children's programming that has parents salivating to enroll their children in yearly. I am an author, international parenting coach, for six years I was a court-appointed special advocate for youth in foster care, I sit on the Governor's Board of Children and Family Services Task Force team, and am a specialty foster parent. I have been dubbed, "The Child Whisperer" by my staff and people enjoy working with and for me.

So reading this book should definitely inspire you because you are learning from an awesome woman whom I've had the pleasure of personally coaching so that story you just read about how I got started, yup, she is putting into practice in her own business now. I love to see how awesome Tammie's creative brain works. When I read the slayers I was like, "brilliant, the student has surpassed the teacher." Be sure to soak up every bit of knowledge she throws out because she is definitely someone who knows how to slay her slayers.

Tameka Anderson

Preface

Isn't it funny how one conversation can set off a spark and drive you to do something that you may have never thought about doing? That's what happened to me. This was not what my third book was supposed to be about! However, life took over and said that this is it, though I do still plan to write the other one!

I remember clearly -- I was at a speaking engagement with my brother and I was talking to one of the ladies that worked there. She mentioned to me that she wanted to write a book and start a business similar to my educational consulting business. And then it happened -- the excuses! When I explained to her how I managed two run two businesses of my own, help with two others, homeschool my children, work as a substitute teacher, and have a husband, she was speechless!

That conversation stacked with me and I couldn't shake it. I had my book all outlined out and was ready to write, but that conversation permeated my every thought. I had to do something with it...and this is it. Enjoy!

Introduction

The purpose and goal of this book is to help you to see that what you think is standing in your way really isn't. It's a matter of how you're using what you have.

It's a matter of you taking action in what you say you want to do.

It's a matter if being willing to step out of your comfort zone.

It's a matter of priority.

You are your own worst enemy and I am here to help you get out of that baby mentality that you have!

Unlike my last book, this book and workbook combo are separate and it's because I want you to be able to revisit the book as much as you need to.

It's time to meet and slay the Slayers that are attacking your headspace.

It's time to Rise, Reclaim, and Evolve!

The Virtuous Business Woman Revisited

As many of my readers know, The Virtuous Business Woman: Inspired by Proverbs 31 was a true labor of love. That was my baby!

I wrote a book centered around Proverbs 31. The thing that gets me is that I wonder if you truly understand who the Virtuous Woman was. Yes, she is a role model for many of us and one that we say want to be, but are you actually taking the steps to even make that happen? You think you cannot be her because...

She's married with children and you are neither. Consider working towards these qualities as preventative maintenance. If you start infusing these attributes into your daily life, what is said of her just might be said of you one day. You prepare for everything else in life – buying a house, starting a business, buying a car, continuing your education – why not prepare for this as well!

She is a go-getter and you are comfortable where you are. Although I don't recommend skipping through the book, I have a chapter written JUST FOR YOU – if this is what you're dealing with. I'll let you read that.

She takes risks and you live in the land of safitude. Life requires that we make risky decisions from time to time, wouldn't you agree? Whether you think about it or not, you make at least one risky decision a day! Don't think so? Have you ever called into work, knowing full well that they need you to come in? Have you ever delayed paying a bill so that you could do something else? Have you gone on a blind date? I can see you nodding your head, thinking, and laughing. You know what I mean!

She has and manages her own business and you are at entry level. I wrote about this too, so I won't say much here. I just want you to understand that you are so much closer than you think!

Now here is the question of the moment: Why are you letting ANY OF THAT stop you? I'm asking that question because I let all of this and more stop me at one point. Let me tell you about it.

I was one who grew up receiving mixed messages. I was told that I was too smart to work for other people, but too weak to pursue the dreams and goals that I had for myself. As I got into the working world, I was always caught doing my own thing and, to be honest, I found myself in trouble. I had jobs that were based on numbers served and not the quality of the relationship with those that I had. I was disciplined for caring, for not checking behind people who knew their jobs, and for not wanting people to be blind sighted by information that would possibly negatively impact their lives. Now, I'm not saying I was perfect. There were times when the discipline was necessary.

In 2007, I tried to start a business. I had everything I needed...and then my biggest cheerleader, help, and business partner died -- my mom. Back into the workforce I went and I was stressed out! At one point, I was so stressed that I lost thirty pounds in about four months. I spent a lot of days in tears because I was in and out of work...until one of the people who told me I was too smart told me about an opportunity I thought I didn't even think I was qualified to get.

It was funny because I ended up being in the very field that others told me that I wasn't strong enough to pursue -- education! And that's half of my current empire now.

I said all of that to let you know that life doesn't have to stand in your way. I built two businesses with $700 and a stack of homemade business cards, people! We'll get into that a little later.

As I end here, I'm issuing you a challenge! Why? It's because this bothers me and I want to see you do better. This isn't about getting you to read or reread the other book--you can if you choose to. It's about you investing in yourself. It's about caring enough about yourself to give yourself a reality check! Will you step up and invest in yourself?

If you're still shaken by what you've read here, that means that you've been visited by one of the Slayers...

Slayer #1: I'm Broke

My first question to you would be this: Are you really?" Sweetheart, do you know how much stuff is out there for you to use, even if only for a limited time? Bye, Felicia! I found what I needed and used it until I could do better. You can do the same, Honey. My mom always told me to use what I had until I could get what I wanted. That still rings true as a business owner or as a woman in general!

As I said in my first chapter, I started both of my businesses with $700 and a stack of homemade business cards. And, when I say homemade, I don't mean I printed them on my printer at home! I mean that I printed them on cardstock, with the gridlines showing, and dared anyone in my house to touch me or make any noise while I cut them out!

I remember the day that I started Choice Home Education Consulting, my homeschool consulting and tutoring business. I paid $99 to take a twelve class on starting a consulting practice. When I finished that class, I had my plan in place. Summer was coming and I knew that was the best time to lay the groundwork for my business. I was aiming for parents who weren't sending their kids back to school the next year.

It was September 15, 2014 at 8:00 AM. I had $700 in cash that I'd taken from the bonus my husband had received, which wasn't much. I knew that I had to get this done, though. My first stop was to my local Cricket Wireless store to get a cell phone for the business because I didn't want my clients to have my personal number. I also knew that I had to list a phone number on my business license.

From there, I went to the County Clerk's office and got my business license, which didn't take as long as I thought it would and didn't cost that much. I filled out the application, paid the fee, and walked out with the license in my hand. I was official and it felt good! The process was so short that I was almost mad that I'd paid for parking in a nearby garage as opposed to waiting for a meter! I couldn't let that get me down…and I didn't.

My third stop was to the bank to open a business checking account. I wanted to money that I made to be separate so that nothing would get messed up. I had all of the paperwork that I needed and walked out with that in less than an hour.

When I got home, I got to work! I took the time to build my website—which I had been running as a free site—and paid for premium features, set up my social media, created the tax accounts that were required –with the help of an accountant friend of my Dad's—, paid for a logo and real promotional materials, and then got something to eat! By 9:30 PM, I was established!

I started paying for vendor tables at events where I knew I could reach those I was looking for. Some spaces were more expensive than others, but had I not done it at all, I would NOT be where I am now. I was fortunate to earn enough from my material sales to make a profit each time I went to an event. I also gained more than money! I made connections with people that helped me to gain exposure. I started being asked to do live events. People were running my ads in their magazines and newsletters. I was getting phone calls from people asking for more flyers because they'd handed them all out. When I made the investment in myself and my business, I saw myself doubling and sometimes tripling what I spent for those spaces!

One of the things that my mentor taught me was about using free trials for things that I needed in my business. Any time I told her about something that I needed and couldn't pay for, she put me on to something that was free, even if it was online free for 30 days, so that I could get going. I soon realized that I was just making excuses. I didn't look at what was available to me. I purposely wouldn't use free trials because I didn't want to think about how I was going to pay for it once the trail was up. Having this mindset messed me up because soon, I found myself not having a choice— I needed it to keep my business moving forward!

What is it that you want to do? What is it going to take for you to get that? Yes, I know that it takes money; however, do you have a plan in place to make that happen? Have you found out whether or not you can make it work for a time until you get some things together?

When I started my second business, Tammie Terrell Mompreneur Coaching, I made my first set of business cards on my printer at the house. How? I made a phone call. My Dad was cleaning his garage out and came across a milk crate full of **UNOPENED PAPER MEDIA**—business card paper, brochure paper, postcard paper—everything that I needed! I spent the money to buy ink and printed business cards and brochures page by page until my ink ran

out. I ended up with 100 business cards and 50 brochures—and it barely cost me anything. Before then, I made my business cards on cardstock, made sure I printed with the gridlines showing, and meticulously cut them out myself! I was preparing for an event and didn't want to go in empty-handed. I knew that something was better than nothing.

I also bartered. I went to the people that could do what I needed, told them what I could do to help them, and then busted my butt to put forth my best effort in order to get what I needed done. Now, I will tell you to be careful with bartering. You can't get everything for free and word gets around fast about women who try to—especially in the business world. How many times have you avoided someone because they were always looking for something for free? EXACTLY! Everyone's time, talent, and work has to paid for!

When I looked for discounts and hookups, I missed out on getting the help that I really needed. I was always sitting back waiting for the price to go down, for a coupon code, etc. I knew that it would help my business, but the price was all wrong—or so I thought. I had to start looking at it from the seller's point of view. This was their business, their baby, their livelihood, and their lifeline. Who was I to expect them to come down simply because I didn't WANT to make that investment? That's what my problem was as a customer.

So, now that we've talked about all of that, I have one question: What's stopping you? Correction: What are you doing to stop yourself, Love?

Yes, it does take money to make money, yet there are ways of getting things done for now until you get going well enough to upgrade what you have out there! Here's my challenge: Make a list of what you need and where you want to get it. Look and see if you can try it before you commit to it. For example, the software I use to book my clients has a 30-day free trial, but I can extend it for 3 days as I need to.

Sweetie, you aren't broke! You just don't know what's out there and it's time that you find out. You're missing out on getting an awesome

START on your vision sitting back talking about what you can't afford to get right now.

Also, being broke is a matter of priorities as well. You will pay for what is important to you and not always look for a handout, hookup, or discount. It all goes back to what I said about people's time and talent being paid for. While you may think someone's price is too high, stop to consider what all goes into the product or service they provide. Even if you do find it at a lower price, cheaper is not always better! You may think that they're just selling their name or their brand and find an off brand, but think about the times when you have wished that you put out the money for the higher product or service!

I also want you to think about a time when you have spent money on something and realized that the money would've been better spent by doing something for your home or business. Now, I'm not saying that you can't do things for yourself or that you have to put what you want on the backburner forever! The point that I'm trying to make is that you have to INVEST IN YOURSELF and in something other than clothes, shoes, purses, accessories, and entertainment. All of this stuff is temporary and you're either going to grow out of it, mess it up, or end up selling it!

Are there ways to invest in your business when you are "broke?" If you're still asking this question after reading all of that, then this Slayer is most definitely attacking your headspace!

When this Slayer is active in your life, you can't see anything wrong with your train of thought. You find yourself getting mad because there is a price involved with everything that you want to do. You get mad when someone tells you that the money that you're about to spend shopping will be better used elsewhere and then you end up begging someone to borrow the money that you would've had if you had given two more seconds' thought to what you are trying to achieve.

If you're really as frustrated as you say you are about your situation, money won't be an issue because you will make it work. I watch men and women alike do it every day. I have come to realize that some don't have it because they don't want it. They don't want to do what it takes to get them to where they want to do be.

As I leave you to go to the workbook, I really want you to think about your relationship with money because that's a big part of it as well. It might mean that it's time to make some changes so that you can have a better handle on things. It's time for you Big Girl Pill, Lady!

Slayer #2: I Don't Have Time

Are you managing your time or are you wasting it? There is a difference between the two. And, if you are real with yourself, you know that you are **WASTING** your time. Think about those days where you stayed in the bed watching TV all day. How did that make you feel? You're good with that? Let me put it like this then: think about those days where you stayed in the bed watching TV all day, only to look up and see that you haven't gotten anything done **ALL DAY** and now you're mad. See, that's what I'm talking about right there.

When was the last time you really looked at how you spend your time every day? It's not something that people like to do, but sometimes we need to give ourselves a reality check because we know that we ain't right!

When you manage your time, you get more than you thought you would have done because you have a plan and aren't afraid to multitask. If you're not good at multitasking, you need to get there. It's not as hard as you think. Do you know what I do while I'm under the hairdryer at the salon? I read, update my business social media pages and blogs, get caught up on emails, pay bills—see where I'm going with this?

While you are on the computer scrolling through Facebook, have a motivational YouTube video playing while you're sitting there reading or use that time to find helpful groups and pages to follow. While you are out and on your way to the store, have an audio book playing on the radio in the car. Are you sitting under the hair dryer at the beauty shop? Read a book that's going to help you get what you are trying to do done. While you're on hold waiting for your call to be answered, put your call on speaker and write out your goals for the rest of the day, week, month, or year. If you're at work and the project you're working on is something that speaks to you, make some notes of how you can use what you're doing in your business. If you're in a meeting and your mind starts to wander a bit, sketch out some ideas for your business. While you're eating lunch, brainstorm what your next move might be.

If you're a mom, what do you do when your kids are down for the night? Yes, I know that you might say that's your time and I'm all for that; however, are you taking advantage of your nights? It's okay to take that time to yourself and just breathe, but you also need to be making moves and making plans to get yourself to the next level.

That is the best time for a mom to work, in my opinion. I tell people all the time that I sleep from midnight to 5:30 AM. Why? It's because—while I am up doing things in the house or for myself—I tackle any business project that I couldn't get to while they are awake. I will scroll through and read or watch all of the stuff that I pinned and saved. I will look at and straighten out my accounting records using the app that I have.

When you have a day off or even a day to yourself, how do you spend it? Getting your hair, nails, and feet done is in order, yes, but in order for you to get to where you say you want to be, use some of that time to find out what it takes for you to get there.

Have you ever dismissed an opportunity that you say you didn't have time for, only to realize that what you chose to do wasn't as important as what you passed up? It's time to put a stop to that because you are **NOT** going to get anything done doing that. It's all about your vision being a priority to you! When your vision is a priority, you become more intentional with your time. You start to ask yourself if what you're about to do is going to get you closer to your goal. Don't be mad because you're being hit with the truth. Take that truth, put it in your purse, and let's keep moving forward.

I was sitting in an event once and a lady started telling me what she didn't have time to do, which is something that I get often. I am going to debunk this Slayer right now because, Honey, you DO have time! If I can do all that I do and still be able to stand at the end of the day, so can you. So, what DO I do?

I substitute teach three to five days a week, tutor six days a week, run a homeschool co-op two days a week, help my best friend and little brother with their businesses and wrote two books within three months of each other! Whew! Okay, so now tell me about what you don't have time to do!

Do I sleep? Yes—from midnight to 5:30 AM CST. Am I on anything? Nope! Am I part Jamaican? Nope, but I have been asked that before. Don't you have a family? That's in the next chapter! Do you get time to yourself? Yes!

All I'm trying to get you to see that you don't have an excuse. That's what this book is about— helping you to see that you're been Slayed, and not in a good way! When this Slayer is and stays active in your life, you don't and won't get ANYTHING done—EVER! Why? It's because you will start to run into people who always need or want something from you. You will encounter people who think that all of your time belongs to them. You will give so much of yourself to others that you will soon realize that you've done absolutely nothing for yourself and your business. You will lose out on clients and networking opportunities because you don't know how to manage your time and energy. You will forever be wondering where the heck the day went.

You may also find yourself saying this because you want to do what you want to do, when you want to do it, how you want to do it, and where you want to do it. Let's add this to the list of things we don't have time for! Yes—THAT! You make time for what you want to do and be successful at doing. I'm sorry if you're taken aback by that, but both you and I know that to be true!

We've all had moments where our friends and family have gotten in our butts about how we spend our time; however, our first instinct is to get offended—not to think about what they're actually saying. You will stand in line for HOURS waiting on a store to open, concert or game tickets, or for something free, but you won't spend that same amount of time working on the business that you say that you want to have. Think about how mad you got when it was finally your turn and what you came for was all sold out or not available where you were! Your whole day is gone and you start thinking about that person who got on to you for not using your time wisely. Uh huh—I've done it, too.

It's not that you don't have time; it's that you won't make time. You won't put entertainment aside for two seconds to take care of business and then you get mad because places are closed, discount codes and specials expire, or all available slots are taken. You can't do stuff when you want to and expect to make progress!

As I said before, this mindset is what you don't have time for. You can work and still have a successful business, but it takes TIME to find out how to make that work. You have to make time to do that. It's not going to show up in a Facebook message, my dear.

You have the time to do anything that you those that you follow do—to a point. The question is if you are willing to give up and delay some things in order to get that done. Are you willing to restructure your day in order to work on your business? For many, if not most, the answer to that question is NO!

You must realize that there is a time and a place for everything and that's not going to change. How long are you going to let your business be on the back burner so that you can do something that uses time that you need to move forward?

You must also realize that you get the same 168 hours that everyone else gets. While you might have "more going on than she does", it's still about managing your time. My coach told me that I need to be strategic and intentional with my time. That means that I spend my time on building relationships with people, keeping up income generating activities and taking care of myself in all aspects.

You can get those in the wrong order and focus on one too much! I spoke about this in The Virtuous Business Woman. I stressed the importance of maintaining the woman without and within. When you only focus on business, self and relationships suffer and vice versa. Again, it's all about managing your time. It's all about balance.

Take control of your time! I have an exercise in the workbook that I want you to take real seriously and I'm going to go ahead and tell you about it. I want you to analyze one day of your time—not an easy request I know. To the best of your ability, I want you to account for every second of a day of your choosing and write down everything you did and how long you spent doing it.

I won't spoil step two…

Slayer #3: I Have a Family

This is one I hear way too much and it irks my eternal soul! **STOP USING YOUR FAMILY AS A CRUTCH, HONEY**! Stop saying what you can't get done because you have kids, a husband, or both! As long as you keep saying that to yourself and others, you will **NEVER** get what you want to do done. Do I have a family? Yes, I do; however, I get up every day and run my business. You wanna know what I found out when I stopped saying that? It was the day I figured out that my family was one of my greatest assets and yours can be, too. Girl, let me tell you what happened!

It was a Tuesday morning and I was taking my daughter to see a pediatric neck specialist. I was on one phone with a client and received a text on my other phone from a friend. My daughter held up the phone so that I could see the message. My friend's aunt wanted to talk to me for homeschool help. I nodded and continued to listen to my client. Next thing I know; my daughter taps me on the shoulder as I'm starting the car.

She had sent my friend a text message that said: "Okay great! I'm on a client call right now, but I'll call her soon." She was able to do that because she'd been watching me and how I spoke, how I wrote—ALL OF THAT! So, let's not use our families as an excuse, okay?

Still not convinced? Let's try this: when I found office space near my house, I took my husband to see it because he has much better visual-spatial capacity than I do and can decorate like the pros! He took a couple of pictures, came home, and got to work. My office is gorgeous and it's all because I used his artistic abilities to furnish and organize my office. When I started writing, he would do read-throughs with me and give me his opinion on my writing. He is also my biggest supporter and investor!

The truth is that you really haven't taken the time to see what gifts are talents are right there in the house with you! Think about the time when someone you know told you to let your family help and the first thing that came to your mind was that they couldn't. Have you allowed them to try? They may not do things exactly the way that you want them and might not completely understand what you want them to do; however, they will be there when no one else will, so consider this to be a teachable moment for all of you.

You say that you want a better life for your family and that's why you are doing what you're doing, yet you sit back every day and talk about what you couldn't get done because they were around. Or, you say that you can't do what you want to do right now because you have to provide for them. I'm going to talk about that in just a minute.

Having a family does not stop you from living your dream. They do not stop you from going after what you say that you want. Instead of seeing them as a reason why you can't, start seeing them as the reason why you need to! Your family should be your motivation and not your excuse to not move forward.

You may have a unique family situation that takes up a lot of your time. I understand that as well—you can still get things done. I am married. Two of our three daughters have language delays and have been diagnosed with autistic tendencies. I am also a homeschool parent and have all three of our girls at home. None of that stops me from running either one of my business nor working another job. You may not be able to do it at the level that you want to until you get some things settled, but you can still work toward your goal! Why should you, you ask? It's because they are watching you. Don't believe me? Go back and read the beginning of this chapter.

Your family is looking to see how you handle things. When they see your sacrifices on their behalf, most times they will step in and help. I've seen that in my own family. I was ironing clothes one night after finally getting our younger girls into bed. Our oldest came up to me and asked me to teach her to iron so that she could help me. It's all about teaching them! I remembered how much I could do at the age of 9 and set out to teach my daughter. I let my husband know where I needed help from him and he stepped up.

Think back to all of the times when you passed on doing something because of your family life. How many times have you regretted saying that, especially when you look back and see that you could've made that work…or your spouse or significant other told you that they would've backed you had you told them about it… or that family member said they would've watched the kids while you took care of that. Yes, I understand that you don't like to ask for help, but Honey, sometimes you have to grit and bear it. As the saying goes, "You have not because you ask not!"

Your family needs to see you still working at the business you want to start, the life you want to have, and the life that you want them to have. I cannot stress this enough! You can't teach them to not give up if you do. You can't expect them to have a strong work ethic if you're cutting corners. You can't expect them to catch the entrepreneurial spirit if you never show it!

I know and understand that not everything I say applies to you. You may be a single parent and not have a stable support system. You can still make things happen! It's just going to take a little more effort and creativity. Do you have an actionable plan in place? Are you using the help that you DO have, no matter how little it may be? It's worth it!

You may say that you don't have a family right now; however, this is something that you need to think about. This is something that you can plan for now. There is nothing wrong with planning ahead and putting things in place to make whatever family transition you need to make in the future a little easier for you.

When this Slayer is active in your life, you allow your family to be a millstone around your neck or a ball and chain instead of a support underneath you that is holding you up so that you can keep going. You will start to intentionally not be around them because you start to feel as though they are keeping you down. You will start to schedule things in a way where you are gone.

Now, I know that all of us aren't like that and are probably mad that someone would ever think that way, but it happens. I encounter moms all the time who want to know how to get more time for themselves or more time for the business because their family like is so demanding. It's all about learning balance and having a family system that allows you to get things done in the way you need them to do so that neither suffers. We'll work on that in the workbook.

So, I'm going to end with this: Is your family really stopping you or are you saying that they are so that those you are talking to don't think badly of you or look down on you because they know you could be doing exactly what you set out to do? Have you had the help that you needed and didn't use it because you didn't feel like getting out there and doing what needed to be done for your vision to become reality? Uh huh…yep!

Slayer #4: I Have a Job

Yes, I understand that, but how do you view your job? Do you see it as you be all end all or as a means to an end? When was the last time you looked at what you did every day and wondered if you could do this on your own? How many of your coworkers have told you that you need to be doing something with the talent that you let shine on the job? Are you listening to them or even to yourself? No? Then, Sweetie, it's time that you started!

I wrote a blog article about this very thing. We get so wrapped up in not liking our jobs that we don't think about the possibilities of making it our own. We would rather go in, do just enough to keep our bosses off of our backs, gossip about everything that's going on, and watch the clock. We think about getting another job and will even use company time to look for another one. Have I been there? Yes, I have, but I used my feelings as motivation.

I became a substitute teacher in 2010 and I used every day as a learning experience. I kept teachers' schedules so that I knew what to expect every day. I wrote down the names of resources that they used that I liked and made copies of things, if allowed. I watched how each school ran. I went into work every day asking thinking about what skill of mine could be honed or perfected on that particular day. That is how I started my line of educational tools! I started creating things that I brought into the classrooms of those schools and had teachers and principals paying me for the lesson plans!

Do you see what I did there? I didn't focus on school policies, kids' behavior, or anything else—I looked at what I could do to make myself more valuable and more marketable on my own. Now, when I go to a school, I'm allowed to bring in my own materials because they already know my stuff works!

I said all of that because I want you to understand that, sometimes, having a job is a catalyst for you to get stuff done! If you know that you don't want to be there, you need to start making moves while you are there. You need to have plans B through Z already in motion, Honey. Trust me! Nothing that you're dreaming about is going to come without action.

The job that you have is meant to motivate you to do more, greater, and better than you are now— whether you believe it or not. You are **NOT** meant to work minimum wage for the rest of your life. Being an entry-level manager or supervisor is not the end for you. Temporary services are not the only places where you can work and have a flexible schedule. Working part-time is not the only way for you to get things done after work.

As you maximizing your days at work? How much are you internalizing? What are you learning every day? Are you paying attention to those teachable moments? How many job duties can you perform outside of your own? And, again I ask, if you lost that job today, could you turn that into a business for yourself? Could you do it while you're still working there?

I cannot tell you how many times I've seen people establish their own businesses while they still had jobs! If you've paid any attention to anything I've said so far, you will now that I am one! I make it work each and every day and Darling, so can you!

It would take me all day to run through just the people that I know who are doing this very thing. You may have a job, but because of your attitude about that job, you could be missing out on what that job could lead to! For example, your boss may want you to take a special training on new software you're going to be using. It's not something that you want to do. You're tired of going to all of these trainings…and then one day you start to really see what all it can do and that they sell it to individuals as well as companies. Can you use that to build your business? I dare you to think about it that way!

I can tell you now that I use many tools in my business that I first learned about working in classrooms. I have been in situations where my knowledge of different programs has saved companies money and got paid for helping them out. You attending that training is not just a "break from work"—it's an unseen investment into your future and I need you to understand that.

Do you save the things that you create for work and craft them into something that you can use for yourself? Do you create things with that thought in mind? What would happen for you if you allowed your mind to entertain the thought of **THAT**?

I know I am filling your head with a lot of personal examples, but I am doing this because I want you to understand that I know what you're going through. I, like many of you reading this, have had a job where everything that I created became their property. I have had to walk away from award winning programs that I'd created because it was a clause in my employment contract. Once I left that job, I vowed that would **NEVER** happen to me again…and it hasn't.

Look at the reports that you're asked to do, the procedures you're asked to follow—everything! Ask yourself this question each and every time something comes across your path— "If I needed this in my business, how would I do it?" Believe me when I tell you that a simple mindset change can make a bigger difference than you think.

It's time to really start analyzing your job. It is an investment into your dream and you don't even see that! What would happen if you started to, though? Yes, you have a job, but Honey, you can have **SO** much more, even within that job if you take the time to just allow yourself to imagine the possibilities. Those mundane tasks that you do every day could be the very things that unlock the treasure that you have buried because you're more focused on what your job is rather than what it could lead to. Your job is a stepping stone and you need to remember that!

This is what I need you to do before you go to the workbook section for this chapter:

- Realize that this is an excuse.
- Listen to people who are telling you that you can have more, better, and greater.

- Get away from those who keep you in and support this excuse pattern and conversation.

- Push yourself to change your mindset about your job.

- Do some soul searching and figure out what you need to do that you're not doing in order to get to the place you haven't gotten to yet.

When this Slayer is active in your life, you will always go to work tired, frustrated, and being ready to go. You will swear that time is either standing still or going backward because you're staring at the clock just that hard. Anything anyone asks you to do at any time will seem like the hardest and most time consuming thing in the world to do and you won't do it at your fullest potential. You will find yourself becoming envious of those who are where you want to be, but you haven't taken the time to do what's necessary to get where they are.

I'm challenging you to change the way that you look at your job. Find someone who is making it happen in the way you are looking forward to and ask for their help. If you can't find anyone, I'm here for you. You'll have to stay with me until the end to find out how to get with me, though.

Slayer #5: My Talent is Just a Hobby

Okay, so you have this talent, right? And, you made money from it, right? Then, this money that you're making is helping you to get things done even though you earn a regular paycheck, right? So, why are you downplaying it like it's nothing. Let me tell you: If people are constantly telling you that you need to do something more with that you're doing or if you make enough money to not spend your paycheck on household expenses, you need to get real serious about whatever you're doing real quick! You're burying your treasure, Honey!

I had a lady to tell me that she makes an extra $2-$3k a month from her "side hustle!" When I asked her why she wasn't using that as a full-time business, she said that it was just that—a side hustle. She didn't understand that her talent was there for a reason. She didn't see the value in it nor the possibilities thereof. She wouldn't even do the research that's necessary to change her mind. She was so focused on her 9 to 5, that she buried it, even though it was making her that much money.

Not everyone can tell this story, but I do know that someone reading this has had moments where they have looked at themselves and wondered if it was possible to do anything else. I'm here to tell you that it is—it's just up to you to want to do more and find out what it's going to take to get there. Let me tell you that there is nothing worse than being a secret....

Let me explain what's going to happen if you continue to bury that. First, that talent will eventually be all that you have for you to make it one day. But, you're not going to see if even then. You'll be finding any and everything else to do but that. You will continue to disregard it because it's not as important to you as it should be. It will be put in your face every single day and you will push it away because you feel like there's something better out there that will allow you to do more. Worse than that, you'll be missing out on the people who are looking for the talent that you possess, but they won't be able to find you because you ain't ready!

That last statement is one of my biggest fears and something that I bear in mind when I think about quitting. For me, the worst thing in the world is to not be available to someone who will need me. Sweetheart, I know how it feels to want things to work. I know how it feels to be reminded of things that I know how to do and push them away only having to come back to them. I'm going to talk about that now.

Second, you're going to be mad because you won't have what you need for that to happen. You will realize that talent is all that you have and that you spent so much time chasing something else that now you have to scramble to get what you need.

You'll be running around frantic and mad because things are out of stock, discontinued, priced higher than it was before, or the store where you usually go for it will be closed. I know that, to some, that will seem extreme, but it most definitely can happen. As the saying goes, "It is better to have it and not need it than to need it and not have it." You have may to replace a few things here and there or may have to pick up a few things that don't have a good shelf life, but you'll have a decent head start.

Third, you're going to do something that you have absolutely no business doing in order to get what you need so that you can work. How many times have you walked into a place, seen someone you know, and asked them what in the world they were doing there? Is that not the most embarrassing moment ever? There are plenty of other ways to make money. You don't have to get involved with something that has you looking over your shoulder in order to establish your place in the world! Yes, you may have to work a few more hours or get a second job to help stabilize things, but even in that you should be watchful of what you get involved in.

Last, you will lose the love that you had for that talent and the light in your eyes will be out permanently. You will do it, but it won't mean anything to you. You'll see it as something to do. Being in that creative space won't be as inspiring as it used to be. When people talk about it, you will roll your eyes and say "It ain't all that. I just threw something together." You'll tune out anyone trying to tell you how skilled and brilliant you are and what good work you do. You will see your talent simply as a means to an end. Why, oh **WHY**, would you do that to yourself? You don't want them kind of problems in your life, believe me!

What you're sitting on and not taking seriously, someone could be looking for. You have to stay on top of your game at all time if you really want what you say that you want. That class that people have been telling you about taking, that YouTube channel people have been telling you to watch and follow—you need to get to looking at it **NOW**! Manage your talents, Honey, don't waste them.

When you're managing your talents, a day does not go by without you watching, reading, or listening to something related to that talent. You're looking for any and every way possible to let others know about the talent that you have. Becoming beyond an expert in it is your goal and you want to show how valuable you are to anyone who comes into contact with you about it! You're always looking for ways to do it better, have a quicker turnaround without sacrificing quality, and pricing it accordingly.

Wasting your talents is the complete opposite of everything that I just said. You brush what people say to the side and allow the job that you have to become your sole focus. You will even go so far as to say that you do what you do so that you can make top dollar at work. Now, that may not sound bad to you, but think about it like this: Is what you're being paid to make them shine with your talent worth the stress attached to it? Plus, it's not yielding what it could be if you stepped out and really showed out on your own. You do watch, read, and listen to things to help you develop it, but you don't have the same drive and zeal that you used to. Then, you'll start listening to people who tell you that you need to keep doing what you're doing, but only because **THEY** are reaping the most benefits from it!

I've said this before, but it bears repeating—I had a neighbor to tell me that I needed to get serious about creating curriculum—I didn't. I took the first job that would allow me to do that and found that everything I created became theirs. Is that you?

When this Slayer is active in your life, this will be you! You will let the fire die out and the talent right along with it. You will put your tools of the trade in a box and stick it in the attic somewhere, in a closet, or you may even sell it. When someone asks you about it, you'll say that you don't do that anymore without having a clear reason why.

I want you to start taking your talents seriously! If you're not sure what you can do, then the workbook exercises will be a springboard for you. I personally don't want to see you allow this mindset to kill the beauty our talent possesses. It's there for a reason. It serves a purpose. Someone wants and needs it. You need to be there and be ready! Why? It could very well be the source of the future that you want for yourself.

Slayer #6: I Don't Know How to Do Anything Else

If you're saying this after reading everything else that's been said, then you really don't know yourself and you need to work on that first. You don't know who you are, what you can do, and what is rare, special, and unique about you and that is a problem much bigger than the Slayers themselves! It means that you have gone through the motions in reading this book if you are still at this point. I digress.

For some, this may actually seem true, but my question to you would be this: Are you willing to learn to do something new or take that one thing you can do and become a beast at it? Are you willing to put together a team of people who can handle the stuff you can't do or don't like to do? If you answered yes to those, then you are without excuse, my dear. Why? It's because that's what it takes to make your dreams work! Don't let this Slayer and the previous one wreak such havoc on your mind and heart.

Being teachable and even coachable is a necessity right now! While you may have that one thing that you totally slay in, never let it be the only thing that you have going for you. It has been said that a millionaire has seven streams of income, so you don't have room for this Slayer in your life at all! I've often heard my pastor say that every man is his teacher. Have you gotten to that point yet? Do you have the desire to learn how to do more, better, and greater? Only you can answer that.

What are you willing to do that make your main thing **THE** main thing? No matter how insignificant you may **THINK** what you do every day is, you can make something of your own out of it. If cooking is your thing, then start small by doing things for family, friends, and coworkers. Make meals for the less fortunate around you. Find ways to get people to eating your food! One of my neighbors put a sign on his gate for breakfast, lunch, and dinner plates—the possibilities are **ENDLESS**! Find out what makes you stand out in what you do and work it.

Just because you see someone else doing what you do doesn't mean that you can't stand out. There is something about the talent that is original to you. You are not meant to reach and help the same people that they are. There is a market out there just for you to tap into. There are things out there that allow for that talent to be honed and perfected that someone else won't want to do, but it will be right in your wheelhouse! They may have the same talent, but they don't have your ability to showcase it and work through it.

Don't look to compete with someone else or try to one up them! It's important for you to focus on YOU and getting yourself together. You don't have time to play the comparison or pity game. Your future is at stake, Lady!

If, during your process, you find that you hit a wall trying to figure out what to do with the knowledge and skill that you have, it may be time to learn something new or branch out into a different area where you can still use that same skill set. All it takes is a little effort, elbow grease, and research! You will never play in the game if you refuse to get off the bench.

I will never forget the day I answered the question many stay at home moms ask—what do you do to make extra money. When I started talking about what I did, I had at least fifteen women messaging me—they were telling me what their experience was, what degrees they had, etc. Why? It is because they wanted to know if there was anything else they could be doing with the skill set and experience that they already had. They were looking for something to help their family go further. Not one of those women sat back and said that they didn't know anything else to do. They were determined to find something and, last time I checked, all of them had done just that!

Another thing you may not have thought about is that there may be a buried talent that you haven't even thought about developing! Yes, I'm talking about that one thing that you know how to do and think is useless. Let me be maybe not the first person to tell you that no talent is useless! You may not know exactly what you to do at this particular moment, but it does serve a purpose. You wouldn't have it in you to do if it didn't.

Maybe it's time to dust that off and see what you have to do to make that more appealing. There are times when our talents clean up just as nicely as we do! You just have to be willing to put the work in behind it to make it shine. Are you up for that challenge? If not, then I urge you to reconsider. You're inviting more Slayers into your life by doing that.

When this Slayer is active in your life, you will literally forget about anything else you know how to do. Anything other than what you do every day will become irrelevant and unimportant. You won't even mention the other things that you know how to do because you will start to fear being ridiculed. Before you know it, all of your confidence in yourself will be done simply because you couldn't get a handle on this. You won't try anything new because you're more concerned with being safe. Taking risks will seem life threatening to you and the thought of doing so just might make you physically ill!

Lady, you know how to do much more than you think you do. It's just that—again—you have done that one thing for so long that you've truly forgotten all that you can do! It's time to start remembering who you are and what you are capable of.

Unfortunately, this usually doesn't come to a head until there is a crisis of some type. I still remember my Mom cooking a full course breakfast in our fireplace because the power was out, we had an electric stove, and we were hungry! She remembered that cast iron skillet set she had and got busy. As we were eating, she looked at us and promised that would never happen again.

When you start to really look at yourself and who you are, get ready to be surprised by all that you've allowed to be pushed to the side and lay dormant for **YEARS**! You're going to start hearing from people who come into your life to remind you of the person that you used to be. Those old interests that you've longed for will return and you'll feel like a kid at Christmas! More importantly, YOU will be back. You'll look in the mirror and see the woman that you forgot existed.

It's high time you got her back, ma'am! The workbook exercises await!

Slayer #7: I'm Good Where I Am

If I had to pinpoint one Slayer as being the **WORST** of the seven, **THIS WOULD BE IT!** Why? It means that you have settled! You have settled for minimum wage, entry level, your talents being a side hustle, and such. You are heading down a dangerous road, Lady, and I need for you to snap back from that. You're cheating yourself, those who support and look up to you, and those who need you.

When you settle, you get mad when you see others who have what you want, but won't make the effort necessary to get. You will talk bad about them to their faces and behind their backs simply because they are showing you what you could have if you stop settling for mediocrity. People will start to ask you why you couldn't do that and you won't have a good reason for it. You'll start to shy away from anyone who is trying to get you out of your comfort zone. Then, you will start thinking about all of the stuff that you did in place of what you should've been doing.

Settling becomes a problem in your home as well. Your children, if you have any, watch you. If they see you accepting any and every thing, they will, too! You will find yourself getting mad at them and saying that they should know better, only to have them to remind you that you took the exact same road. Tears will fill your eyes as you try to explain to them why what they're doing isn't good enough and how they are worth more. They will ask you why you didn't do more.

As a parent now or in the future, this is NOT something you want to have on you. It will cause problems between you and those you love because they will tell you that you've lowered yourself from the ambitious go-getter they used to know. Is that something you really want to deal with?

This is one of the reasons why I love Whitney Houston's song "On My Own." She speaks in the voice of a woman who settled, but realized that she needed to do better. She looked at her life and knew that it wasn't for her anymore. I don't have to ask if that's you because I know it is.

How many people have told you that what you're doing is okay but you could be doing better? It's time that you start listening. As the saying goes, "Greatness is in you…you better act like it!" You don't have time to settle, Honey. There is too much in this world for you to do and it won't get done with you being complacent.

Or, you may be in a much better state than that. Corner office. Six figures. Personal assistant. Expense account. Tailor-made everything. Then, you start to feel like your right shoe is on your left foot! You're making things happen day in and day out and it's not enough. You have shattered the glass ceiling into a million pieces and have gained presidential level notoriety, yet you go home asking yourself what you have you really accomplished. You start to wonder if what you're into really matters in the end. When people ask, you tell them about the glitz and glamour that is your life, but those feelings just won't die.

And then, the unthinkable happens—somebody walks up to you and say, "Hey, Lady. Are you okay?"

Your stomach and head starts to hurt at the same time. You feel dizzy and lightheaded. Every wall that you put up is breaking down. With the last little bit of tact and strength you have left, you say, "I'm good." No, Sweetheart, you're not! The problem is that you didn't see that until it was too late.

First of all, you should be grateful that someone noticed enough to even ask you because it shows that they truly do care about you. Second, realize that this, too, is indeed settling! Settling for success at the expense of your physical, mental, spiritual, or emotional well-being is just as bad as lowering your standards. What is success if you're too miserable to enjoy it?

You can be a miserable success and I don't want that for you. You shouldn't want that for yourself because it will soon show. You'll find yourself fighting to maintain that level of productivity that everyone expects of you. Fatigue and illness will come up on you suddenly. What used to fire you up doesn't work anymore, but you still say "I'm good." You're not. You've settled to…even though it's better than what I talked about before. You're looking for more and don't know where to find it.

I challenge you to take the time to really evaluate yourself and what "I'm good" really means in your life. Don't look at your bottom line. Don't look at the material things that surround you. Put aside the accolades that you get all day every day. Are you really "good?"

When this Slayer is active in your life, "I'm good" is your answer to everything, good or bad. You could lose your job or business today and, if someone asks you how you feel, you'll say it before you even realize it. You will stay in a business relationship that is draining the everlasting life out of you. Your level of tolerance will be taken advantage of because you don't stand up for yourself and say what you do or don't want. People will say and do things around you simply because you say you're "good."

Be careful with that phrase because it can do more damage than you know. Realize that there is always room for improvement and that no one has "arrived," no matter what level of success they seem to show. Recognize the fact that you need to use every new, God-given day to do more, better, and greater.

Becoming complacent will make it harder for others to be around you, too. No one wants to hang around or be associated with anyone who is not trying to better themselves, whether they are at the top already or they are starting from the bottom.

At this point, it's time to really look deep inside of you and Slay the Slayers that are running rampant in your life. The exercises here aren't easy ones because you're really going to have to knock down some pretty high and thick walls to get what you need.

In closing, I want to thank you for taking this journey with me. I know that it wasn't an easy one. If you are still in deep thought, then I've done my job. If you feel like you've got a handle on it, keep your guard up because they will rear their ugly, trifling heads again. The Slayers exist to take you out. They are meant to kill you and your vision and slowly.

It is my hope that you're ready to do battle…

Now What Do I Do?

• You've met the Slayers. Worrisome, aren't they?

• You know which ones are running rampant and trying to take you out. What are you gonna do about it?

• Now, it's time for you to put action behind it! If you don't, they will stay!

• I've put together a worksheet for each Slayer and I want you to work through them. I also included a few things you can do throughout the week in order to keep them at bay.

• Peel back all the layers that you put on every day to make it seem like all is well. We just talked about being complacent, so don't even!

• I originally wanted the worksheets and exercises to come after each chapter in this book, but I changed my mind because I wanted to make sure that you had your full arsenal, so I made them separate.

- I didn't want you to stop until it was clear that you knew exactly what you were up against.

It's up to you now, Lady!

About Tammie and TTMC

Hey, Lady! My name is Tammie and I am the creator of Tammie Terrell Mompreneur Coaching (TTMC). My goal is three fold: Rise. Reclaim. Evolve! I am here to help you to Rise above your frustration, Reclaim your life and the talents you've either allowed to lie dormant or use to further the cause of others, and Evolve into the woman who is free to transform those talents into a treasure—a God-honoring business.

More importantly than all of that, I am a mother like many of you reading this book. When I'm not building my empire and plotting world domination, I am usually wrestling around with my husband and three girls or driving through the streets of my hometown, Memphis, TN.

Like you, I started my entrepreneurial life after being tired, frustrated, and waiting for the day to have and run my own. As a matter of fact, that's how my journey started. Like you, I waited for that final straw and it came!

Looking back, I can remember the Facebook conversation that led to my starting a second business—this one. TTMC exists to help you to understand that life is not in your way—you are! I'm here to help you to understand what having a God-honoring business really means and that it is possible, even in today's world. I want to help you get rid of the excuses that are plaguing you and that's why I wrote this book.

Whether you are already in the trenches or you're standing on the sidelines looking over to see if you want to get involved, I'm here for you! My programs are designed to help from the inside out. I help you figure out why you're stuck. I listen and encourage you to listen to what you're saying about yourself. I show you that it's possible to carry your faith with you throughout your business dealings. I help you to analyze your talents and see them for the gems that they are!

I believe in you so much that, if you're getting this book outside of being enrolled in my program, I want to offer you a complimentary 30-minute hot seat coaching call to discuss slaying the Slayer of your choice! Visit my website at http://www.tammieterrellmompreneurs.com today!

www.ingramcontent.com/pod-product-compliance
Lightning Source LLC
Chambersburg PA
CBHW060405190526
45169CB00002B/767